Who Forged This Document?

Crime-Solving Science Projects

Enslow Elementary
an imprint of
Enslow Publishers, Inc.
40 Industrial Road
Box 398
Berkeley Heights, NJ 07922
USA

http://www.enslow.com

ROBERT GARDNER

Enslow Elementary, an imprint of Enslow Publishers, Inc.

Library of Congress Cataloging-in-Publication Data

Gardner, Robert, 1929–
    Who forged this document? : crime-solving science projects / Robert Gardner.
      p. cm. — (Who dunnit? Forensic science experiments)
    Includes bibliographical references and index.
    Summary: "Presents several forensic science experiments using forgery detection skills. Includes science project ideas and crimes to solve"—Provided by publisher.
    ISBN 978-0-7660-3246-0
    1. Forgery—Juvenile literature. 2. Forensic sciences—Juvenile literature. 3. Forensic sciences—Experiments—Juvenile literature. 4. Science projects—Juvenile literature. I. Title.
    HV6675.G36 2011
    363.25'65—dc22

                                           2008050063

Printed in the United States of America

092009 Lake Book Manufacturing, Inc., Melrose Park, IL

10 9 8 7 6 5 4 3 2 1

To Our Readers: We have done our best to make sure all Internet Addresses in this book were active and appropriate when we went to press. However, the author and the publisher have no control over and assume no liability for the material available on those Internet sites or on other Web sites they may link to. Any comments or suggestions can be sent by e-mail to comments@enslow.com or to the address on the back cover.

♻ Enslow Publishers, Inc., is committed to printing our books on recycled paper. The paper in every book contains 10% to 30% post-consumer waste (PCW). The cover board on the outside of each book contains 100% PCW. Our goal is to do our part to help young people and the environment too!

Photo credits: Enslow Publishers, Inc., p. 35; Shutterstock, all other photos.

Illustration credits: © 2009 by Stephen Rountree (www.rountreegraphics.com), Figures 1, 2, 3, 8, 9, 10; Kenneth G. Rainis, Figures 4, 5, 6, 7.

Cover photo: Shutterstock

Contents

Who Dunnit?
Forensic Science Experiments

Experiments with a 🎗 symbol feature **Ideas for a Science Fair Project.**

Introduction

Crime scene . . . forensic evidence . . . fingerprints . . . DNA. You probably hear these words often. Forensic science television programs show scientists solving crimes. Perhaps you would like to try it, too. But what *is* forensic science?

Forensic science is used to solve crimes. The findings can be used in court. This means scientists have to be very careful when they collect evidence and investigate crimes. Evidence collected at a crime scene can put a person in jail. But some people have been found innocent and released from prison as a result of forensic evidence. In this book, you will learn about and practice some of the skills used by forensic detectives.

Entering a Science Fair

If you have to do a science fair project, doing one about forensic science and documents can be a lot of fun. Some experiments in this book are marked with a 🏵 symbol. They are followed by ideas for science fair projects. But judges at science fairs like experiments that are creative. So do not simply copy an experiment from this book. Expand on one of the suggested ideas. Or think up a project of your own.

The Scientific Method

Scientists try to understand how things work. They make careful observations. They do experiments to answer questions. Nearly all scientists use the scientific method. They: (1) observe a problem; (2) form a question; (3) make a hypothesis (a best-guess answer to the question); (4) design and do an experiment to see if the hypothesis is true; (5) analyze the results of the experiment; (6) if possible, form conclusions; (7) accept or reject the hypothesis.

Scientists share their findings. They write articles telling other scientists about their experiments and results.

How do you begin a project you can use in a science fair? You start by noticing something that makes you curious. So you ask a question. Your question might arise from an earlier experiment, something you saw, something you read, or for another reason.

Once you have a question, you can make a hypothesis— a possible answer to the question. Then you can design an experiment. The experiment will test your hypothesis. For example, suppose your question is "Did suspect X write an illegal check?" Your hypothesis might be that suspect X wrote the check. To test your hypothesis, you collect writing samples from X and several other possible suspects. You then compare the written samples with the same words found on the check. If X's writing matches that on the check, your hypothesis was probably correct. You might conclude that X wrote the check. If X's writing does not match the writing on the check, you will need to develop a new hypothesis.

Your experiment might lead to other questions. These questions will need new experiments. That's the nature of science!

Safety First

To do experiments safely always follow these rules:

1 Always do experiments under **adult** supervision.

2 Read all instructions carefully. If you have questions, check with the adult.

3 Be serious while experimenting. Fooling around can be dangerous to you and to others.

4 Keep your work area clean and organized. When you have finished, clean up and put materials away.

Indented Writing and Handwriting

Criminals sometimes write things down when they are planning their crime. Kidnappers write ransom notes. Bank robbers write plans for their robbery. Forgers write and sign checks for other people's money. Sometimes, they make the mistake of leaving their notes at the crime scene! Forensic scientists may use such writing as evidence in court.

In this chapter you will learn about indented writing. It can help solve crimes. You will see how handwriting can be analyzed and used as evidence. Then you will try to solve a crime that involves writing.

🎗 1-1 Indented Writing

1 Ask a friend to use a ballpoint pen to write something on a notepad. It might be a shopping list. It could be a reminder to do something. Do not look at the writing. The person who does the writing should tear off the page with the writing. The notepad should be left for you to examine.

2 Hold the pad at an angle to the light from a lamp. Turn it slowly. You will see that the writing has indented the paper. You will probably be able to read what was written on the missing page.

Surprise the person who did the writing. Tell him or her what was written.

If you have difficulty reading the indented writing, try this: Find a pencil with soft lead. Gently slide the side of the pencil lead back and forth across the indentations. The lead will not darken the indentations. You should see white writing against the dark background.

THINGS YOU WILL NEED:

- a friend to write
- ballpoint pen
- notepad
- lamp
- pencil with soft lead

Ideas for a Science Fair Project

- Will indented writing be easier to see on damp paper? Do an experiment to find out.

- What are watermarks? Where can they be found? What makes them visible?

Electrostatic Detection Apparatus (ESDA)

Even very faint indentations can be made visible with the Electrostatic Detection Apparatus (ESDA). The electrical properties of paper are changed when it is compressed. To see indented writing, the paper is placed on the ESDA. It is then covered with a thin plastic sheet. These are placed between electrically charged plates. The paper becomes charged, but the charge pattern is different where the paper is indented. The paper is then sprayed with toner (small carbon particles) and fine glass bits that stick to the electric charges on the indentations. This makes the writing visible.

Police use the ESDA as well as visible indented writing to solve crimes. Indented writing is valuable evidence. It can be used to solve crimes and to convince a jury of a defendant's guilt.

🎗 1-2 Handwriting

No two people have the same fingerprints. And no two people have the same handwriting. However, matching fingerprints is much easier than identifying handwriting.

Here are some things to look for when trying to identify someone's handwriting.

- Do the letters slant to the right or to the left? (See Figure 1a.) Left-handed people's writing often slants to the left.

- Do the letters slant a lot or just a little? (See Figure 1b.)

- Are there loops in letters such as f, g, h, j, k, l, q, and y? (See Figure 1c.)

- Is the writing smooth, jagged, or by a trembling hand? (See Figure 1d.)

- Are some letters written with flourishes or in an unusual way? Are there unusual spaces between letters? (See Figure 1e.)

THINGS YOU WILL NEED:

- paper
- pens and pencils
- tracing paper
- ruler
- 4 or 5 classmates or members of your family

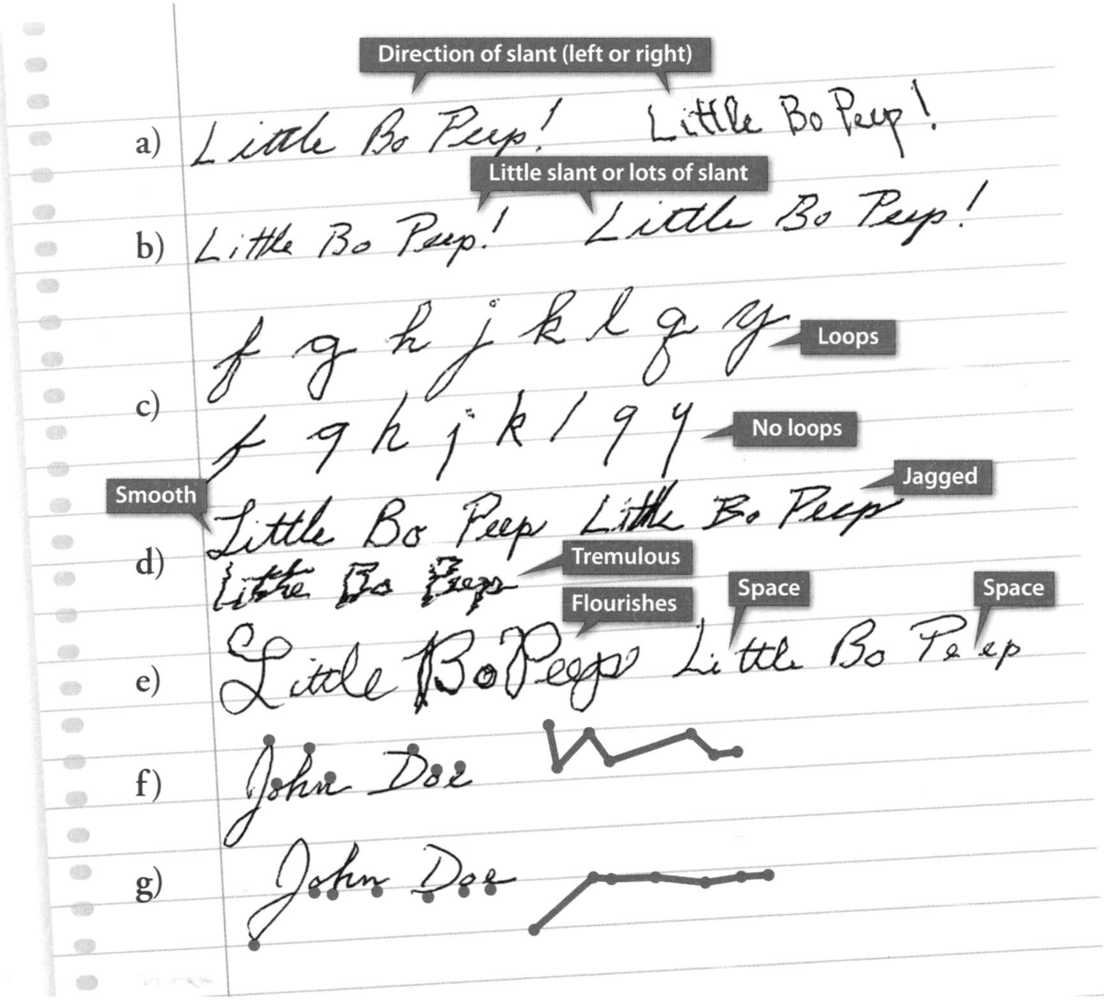

a) *Little Bo Peep!*   *Little Bo Peep!*

Direction of slant (left or right)

b) *Little Bo Peep!*   *Little Bo Peep!*

Little slant or lots of slant

c) f g h j k l g y

Loops

f g h j k l g y

No loops

d) *Little Bo Peep Little Bo Peep*

Smooth   Jagged

Little Bo Peep

Tremulous

e) *Little Bo Peep*   *Little Bo Peep*

Flourishes   Space   Space

f) *John Doe*

g) *John Doe*

Figure 1 a-e) Things to look for when you examine handwriting
f-g) Use dots to form a pattern for handwritten words.

You can also do what handwriting experts do. Make patterns from the handwriting.

1 Write your name on a sheet of paper.

2 Place a sheet of tracing paper over your name.

3 Use a pencil to make dots on the tracing paper. Put the dots at the highest point of each letter in your name.

4 Use a ruler to connect the dots. It will form a pattern like the one shown in Figure 1f.

5 Repeat the process, but this time place a dot at the lowest point of each letter in your name. Again, use a ruler to connect the dots. It will form a pattern like the one shown in Figure 1g.

6 Ask friends or family members to write you brief messages. Have each person sign his or her message. Then ask them to choose one person to write you an unsigned message.

7 Examine the handwriting on all the messages carefully. Use what you have learned. Who wrote the unsigned message?

Ideas for a Science Fair Project

- Write your name on a sheet of paper. Give the paper to someone. Ask him or her to try to forge your signature (write your name so that it looks like your signature). Use handwriting analysis to show that it is a forgery.

- Does a person's handwriting change with age? Design an experiment to find out. (Hint: A parent or grandparent may have letters, essays, or notes they wrote many years ago.)

- Can you tell a girl's handwriting from a boy's? Design experiments to find out.

- Can you always tell from handwriting whether or not a person is left-handed? Design an experiment to find out.

Who Dunnit? A Crime to Solve

An army general has been kidnapped by terrorists. The ransom note in Figure 2a was sent to the President.

Four suspects have been arrested. You are called to Washington by the FBI because you are a handwriting expert. You know that a suspect who is guilty might try to disguise his handwriting. Consequently, you do not ask each of them to rewrite the ransom note. Instead, you ask each suspect to write lengthy articles that you dictate.

You then cut out words from each suspect's lengthy writing. The words you cut out match those in the ransom note. You have carefully put those words together to match the ones in the ransom note. You have done this for each suspect. The results are shown in Figure 2b.

Carefully examine the notes in Figure 2b. Did one of the suspects write the ransom note? If you think so, which suspect is it? What evidence do you have to support your conclusion?

THINGS YOU WILL NEED:
Figure 2

a) RANSOM NOTE

Mr. President: To get your general back put $10,000,000 in a sealed suitcase. Send it on unarmed Air Force One to Paris. Further instructions will follow after plane lands in Paris.

b) SUSPECT 1

Mr. President: To get your general back put $10,000,000 in a sealed suitcase. Send it on unarmed Air Force One to Paris. Further instructions will follow after plane lands in Paris.

SUSPECT 2

Mr. President: To get your general back put $10,000.00 in a sealed suitcase. Send it on unarmed Air Force One to Paris. Further instructions will follow after plane lands in Papis.

SUSPECT 3

Mr. President: To get your general back put $10,000,000 in a sealed suitcase. Send it on unarmed Air Force One to Paris. Further instruction will follow after plane lands in Paris.

SUSPECT 4

Mr. President: To get your general back put $10,000,000 in a sealed suitcase. Send it on unarmed Air Force One to Paris. Further instructions will follow after plane lands in Paris.

Figure 2 a) The ransom note sent to the President.
b) Handwritten words of the four suspects put together to re-create the ransom note.

Inks, Chromatography, and Invisible Inks

You have seen how handwriting can be used as evidence. Ink used to write messages can also be evidence. Forensic document examiners need to know how to identify different inks and different papers. You can start to learn about them, too.

Sometimes there is nothing to be seen on a piece of paper, but there is still a message there. How can this be? The answer 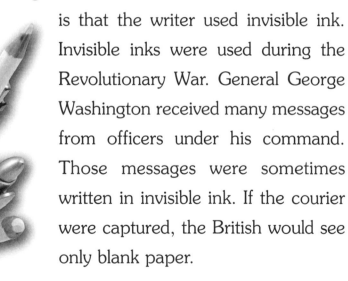 is that the writer used invisible ink. Invisible inks were used during the Revolutionary War. General George Washington received many messages from officers under his command. Those messages were sometimes written in invisible ink. If the courier were captured, the British would see only blank paper.

2-1 Separating the Colors in Ink: Chromatography

Chromatography is the combination of two Greek words: *chroma* (which means "color") and *graphein* (which means "to write"). Chromatography allows you to separate colored chemicals in inks.

Paper is made of small fibers pressed tightly together. There are small spaces between the fibers. When paper towels absorb water, the water goes into the spaces between the fibers. Chromatography works because of these small spaces between paper fibers. Liquids "climb" up through the tiny spaces. Let's see how it works.

THINGS YOU WILL NEED:

- black felt-tip pens of different brands
- fountain pens with black water-soluble ink
- water
- long tray or plastic dish
- long stick or ruler
- books or bricks
- white coffee filters or blotting paper
- scissors
- ruler
- tape
- If air is dry, you may need a tall jar and aluminum foil
- rubbing alcohol

1 Collect several different brands of black felt-tip pens. Collect several different fountain pens with black ink as well.

2 Add about 2.5 cm (1 in) of water to a long tray or plastic dish. Fix a long stick or ruler about 15 cm (6 in) above the water. You can use books or bricks to support the stick, as shown in Figure 3a.

3 Cut some strips from white coffee filters or blotting paper. The strips should be about 15 cm (6 in) long and 2.5 cm (1 in) wide. Cut one strip for each pen.

4 Use scissors to make one end of each strip arrow-shaped (see Figure 3b).

5 Just above the arrow head on one strip, draw a black line with one of the pens.

6 Use tape to hang the strip with the ink line from the long stick (Figure 3c). Only the tip of the arrow should touch the water. The ink line must stay above the water. Place the pen used to mark the strip next to the strip, as shown in Figure 3c.

7 Mark each remaining strip with a different pen. Hang each strip from the long stick. Be sure that only the tip of the arrow

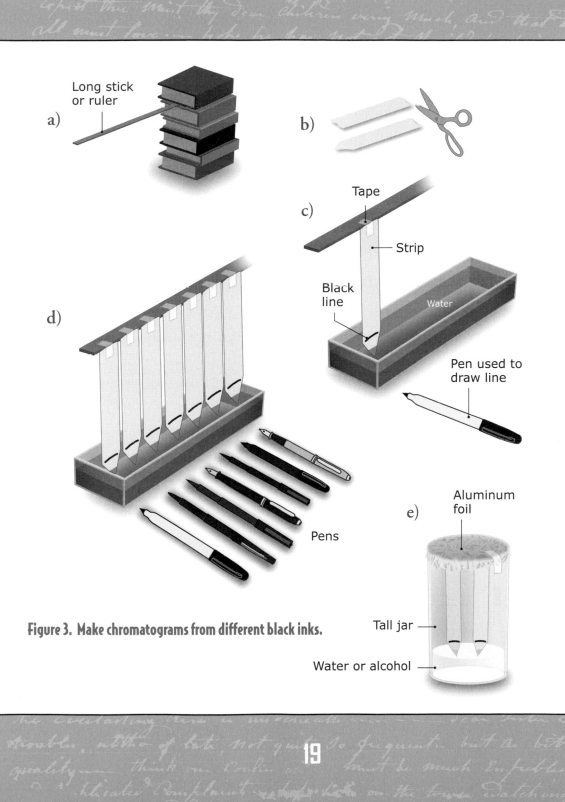

Figure 3. Make chromatograms from different black inks.

touches the water. Place the pen used to mark each strip next to the strip, as shown in Figure 3d.

8 Water will move up the strips. The water will carry the colors upward. The heavier colored chemicals will move slower than the lighter ones. This will cause the colors to separate. What colors were in the ink of each brand of pen?

9 Sometimes the air is very dry. The water evaporates before it carries the ink very far. Then the colors are not separated. If the air is dry, hang the strips in tall jars (see Figure 3e). Cover the jar with aluminum foil. The foil will prevent the water from evaporating.

10 Some inks won't dissolve in water. Colors in such inks will not move up the strip. For such inks, use rubbing alcohol in place of water.

Ideas for a Science Fair Project

- Do food colorings contain more than one colored chemical? Do experiments to find out.

- Do other colored inks (blue, green, red, etc.) contain more than one colored chemical? How about India ink?

An Ink Library

The International Ink Library is controlled by the United States Secret Service. The library has information about the chemicals found in more than 6,000 inks. The Bureau of Alcohol, Tobacco, Firearms, and Explosives National Laboratory (ATF Laboratory) has chromatograms, similar to the ones you made, from more than 3,000 different inks. These chromatograms can be compared to those produced from evidence collected by the police. Many companies that make inks also record the date that an ink was first manufactured. In several cases, this information was used to show that a fake dated document was dated before the ink on the document even became available.

Chromatography was used in a case involving a bomb sent through the mail. The chromatogram showed that the ink on the address matched the ink in the pen of a suspect. The suspect was convicted and sentenced to life in prison.

🎗 2-2 Invisible Inks

Pretend you are one of George Washington's lieutenants. You can send an invisible message to a friend, parent, or other family member.

THINGS YOU WILL NEED:

- **an adult**
- lemon juice
- saucer
- flat toothpick
- white paper
- friend, parent, brother, or sister
- candle
- candleholder
- kitchen sink
- tweezers or tongs
- matches

1 Pour a small amount of lemon juice into a saucer. The lemon juice is your invisible ink.

2 The wide end of a flat toothpick can be your "pen." Dip the "pen" into the lemon juice. You will need to dip the pen often. Write a short invisible message on a small piece of paper.

3 Give the message to your friend or family member. Ask them to put a candle in a candleholder and place it in a kitchen sink.

4 Hold the paper with tweezers or tongs. **Under adult supervision**, light the candle. Then move the paper back and forth, keeping it well above (not in) the candle flame. The message will slowly appear. **If the paper starts to burn, drop it in the sink.**

 ## Ideas for a Science Fair Project

• Can other fruit juices be used as invisible ink? Do experiments to find out.

• Can sugar dissolved in water be used as invisible ink? Do an experiment to find out.

• Can saliva be used as invisible ink? Do an experiment to find out.

Who Dunnit? A Crime to Solve

A plan to help a convict escape from prison was found in a trash container. The plan was written in black ink using a Sheaffer fountain pen. A suspect was arrested shortly after the crime. He had a Sheaffer fountain pen containing black ink in his shirt pocket. You made a chromatogram from that pen's ink (Figure 4a). You compared your chromatogram with standards from a number of different pens (Figure 4b).

Did the ink in the suspect's pen match any of the standards? If so, was the standard from a Sheaffer fountain pen?

If the inks match, could this evidence alone prove the suspect is guilty? If not, what other evidence would be useful?

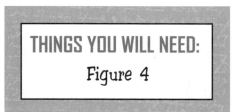

THINGS YOU WILL NEED:
Figure 4

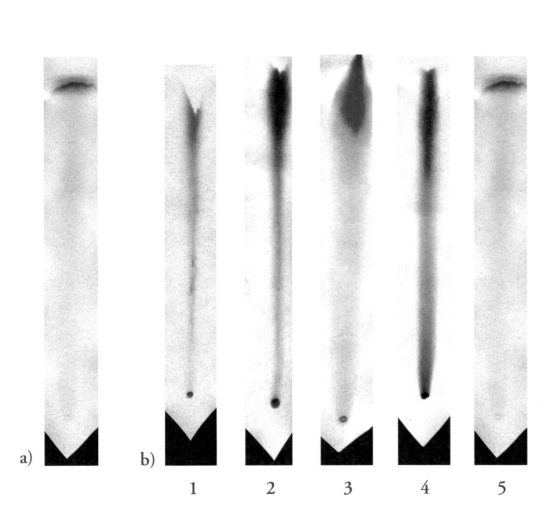

4a) Chromatogram made from the suspect's fountain pen.
 b) Standard chromatograms for various fountain pens: (1) Uniball–blue ink; (2) Uniball–black ink; (3) Pilot–blue ink; (4) Pilot–black ink; (5) Sheaffer fountain pen–black ink.

Identifying Paper, Putting Pieces Together

As you learned in Chapter 2, paper is made of fibers that have been pressed together. They can be cotton or wood fibers, or both kinds. Wood fibers are used in less expensive paper, such as newspaper. Fibers from cotton rags are used to make fine writing paper. Less expensive writing paper has a mixture of wood and cotton fibers. Water and alcohol are attracted to the fibers and will move into the small spaces between the fibers. As you have seen, this property makes chromatography possible.

Sizing is a gel made of glue, wax, or clay. It is used to coat writing paper and art paper. The sizing fills the spaces between the fibers. It makes the paper smooth. And it prevents ink from feathering, or spreading. Ink feathers as it moves along unsized fibers (see Figure 5).

Fine writing paper is sized. It usually has a watermark that identifies the manufacturer (see Figure 6). United States paper money also has watermarks. Hold a five-dollar bill up to the light. You will see a watermark near the lower right-hand corner of the bill. It is the face of President Abraham Lincoln. His face is also printed clearly at the center of the bill.

Figure 5. Ink written on newspaper and other unsized paper will feather (spread) as it seeps between fibers in the paper. The writing will not have a sharp edge.

Figure 6. Hold the paper so light shines through it. If there is a watermark, it will be lighter than the rest of the paper.

3-1 Identifying Paper

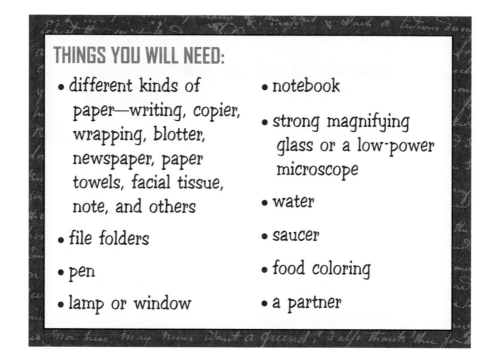

THINGS YOU WILL NEED:

- different kinds of paper—writing, copier, wrapping, blotter, newspaper, paper towels, facial tissue, note, and others
- file folders
- pen
- lamp or window
- notebook
- strong magnifying glass or a low-power microscope
- water
- saucer
- food coloring
- a partner

1 Collect different kinds of paper—writing, copier, wrapping, blotter, newspaper, paper towels, facial tissue, note, and others. Try to find at least two sheets of each kind. Put the different kinds in separate folders. Write the type of paper on each folder.

2 Hold each different kind of paper up to the light from a lamp or window. Does light go through some sheets better than others?

3 Feel the papers. Are some smoother than others? If so, which is the smoothest? Roughest? Record your results.

4 Make a small tear near the corner of a sheet of each kind of paper. Examine the tear with a strong magnifying glass or a low-power microscope. You may see wood or cotton fibers like those in Figure 7. Cotton fibers may be as long as 18 mm (1.8 cm). Wood fibers are shorter, less than 4 mm. Which kinds of paper do you think are mostly wood fibers? Which are mostly cotton? Which are a mix of cotton and wood?

5 Pour some water into a saucer. Add a drop of food coloring. Touch the torn edge of one of the papers to the colored water. Look at the paper through a magnifying glass. Watch the water go into the paper. Does the water go into some kinds of paper faster than others? If so, why do you think some paper absorbs water faster than others?

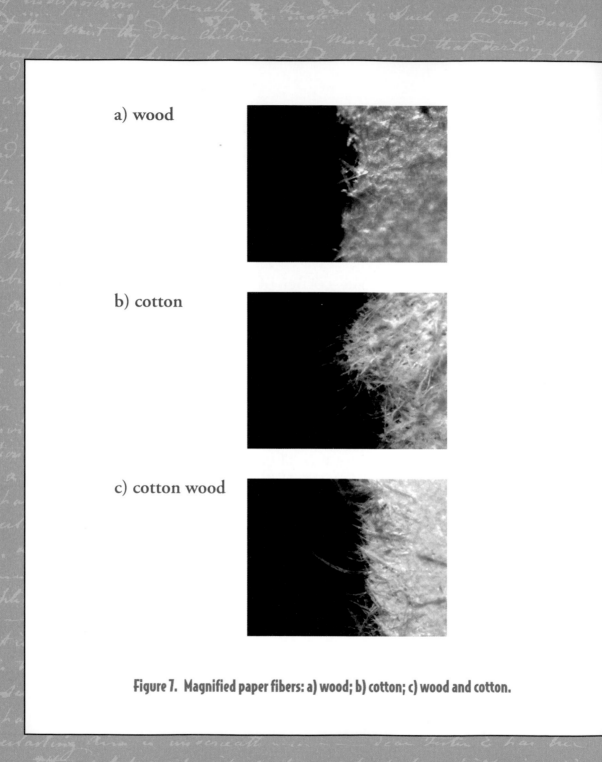

Figure 7. Magnified paper fibers: a) wood; b) cotton; c) wood and cotton.

6 Use a pen to write on each kind of paper. Examine the writing with a magnifying glass. Does the ink look different on some papers than on others?

7 Give the second sheet of each kind of paper to a partner. Ask that person to write a note on one of the sheets. You are not to be present when the note is written.

8 The paper with the note is to be returned to you. Try to identify the kind of paper on which the note is written.

How might forensic scientists use paper to solve a crime?

✿ Idea for a Science Fair Project

Investigate how paper is made. Then see if you can make paper using materials in your home.

3-2 Torn Messages

Criminals may tear messages, plans, maps, photographs, and other evidence into small pieces. Sometimes the pieces can be put back together like a jigsaw puzzle.

1 Ask permission to look at the contents of a wastebasket.

2 Search for documents that have been torn into pieces. If there are none, ask someone to tear some for you. He or she might tear apart a picture, a letter, a bill, an ad from a magazine, or something else. The person should not tell you what was torn into pieces.

3 Now comes the hard part! Try to put the torn pieces back together. If there are glossy pieces, separate the glossy paper from the rest. Pull out the large pieces first. Then separate smaller pieces. Finally, try to piece the documents back together. Can you fit the pieces together to make a sensible document or picture?

THINGS YOU WILL NEED:
- wastebasket with documents that have been torn into pieces, or someone who will tear some for you

Who Dunnit? A Crime to Solve

A bank was robbed. One of the bank's tellers saw the license plate of the getaway car. The next day police found the abandoned car. On the car's floor they found a note that had been cut into pieces. The pieces are shown in Figure 8. You have been asked to put the pieces together.

1 Use a copier or scanner and printer to make a copy of Figure 8.

2 Using scissors, carefully cut out the pieces from the copy. **DO NOT CUT THIS BOOK!**

3 Put the pieces together so that the words make sense. What message was written? To whom was the message sent?

4 Having put the pieces together, what would you suggest the police do next?

THINGS YOU WILL NEED:

- Figure 8
- copier or scanner/printer
- scissors

Figure 8. Pieces of a note found in an
abandoned getaway car.

Forgery, Counterfeiting, and Money

Some criminals make illegal copies of real money. This is called counterfeiting. They try to use the counterfeit money to buy things. The United States Department of the Treasury prints paper money (bills, or banknotes). They print money with values of $1, $5, $10, $20, $50, and $100. Each bill has the picture of a historical person on the front. The treasury works very hard to make it difficult to copy their paper money. But some criminals try their best to make counterfeit bills. They hope people will think the bills are genuine.

Other criminals try to get rich by making and selling forged documents. They might try to sell someone a fake signature of Abraham Lincoln. They might also try to go to the bank and cash a check that is not theirs. They forge the other person's signature on the check.

🏵 4-1 Real or Counterfeit?

How can you tell if paper money is real or counterfeit?

1 Look carefully at a twenty-dollar bill printed after 2003. (You can find a date near the bottom of the bill.) Use a strong magnifying glass. Can you see that the bill is made of fibers? Do they look like wood or cotton fibers?

2 There is an off-center portrait of President Andrew Jackson on the bill. It has lots of lines. These lines are very difficult to copy, even with computers and color copiers or printers.

3 Hold the bill up to the light. Look for a watermark of Jackson's face. It is on the right side of the bill. Can you see the watermark from both sides of the bill?

4 A green or gold "20" is in the lower right-hand corner of the bill. It darkens when viewed from a sharp angle.

5 Microprinting (tiny letters) of *USA* and *20* can be found. They are within the number 20 in the lower left-hand

> **THINGS YOU WILL NEED:**
> - $20 bill
> - strong magnifying lens

corner of the note. You will need a strong magnifying glass to see them. Microprinted *The United States of America* and *USA 20* can be found to the right of the same *20*.

6 Use the magnifier to find a few small colored fibers within the paper.

7 Look for the serial number, which is on the upper left and lower right of the bill. There will be both letters and numerals in the number. The serial numbers on each bill of the same denomination will be different.

Ideas for a Science Fair Project

- Examine other paper currency—$1, $5, $10, $50, and $100 bills. What steps have been taken to make it difficult to counterfeit this money?

- Ask the bank manager to show you how they detect counterfeit money. What do they do when they find fake money? Ask a bank or the local police department for permission to exhibit photos of counterfeit bills and show why the money is counterfeit.

Discovery of a Counterfeiting Scheme

Crime stoppers are people who know about a crime and report it. In June 2000, a detective in Pueblo, Colorado, received a call from a crime stopper. The call led to the arrest of Jerimiah Hall. A search of his home revealed counterfeit bills of various values. A computer and color printer had been used to make the fake money. All the bills of the same denomination had the same serial number. He was charged with forgery.

The public was warned to look for counterfeit money with the serial numbers Hall had used. They were also told that the paper would feel different from real money.

4-2 Checking on Checks

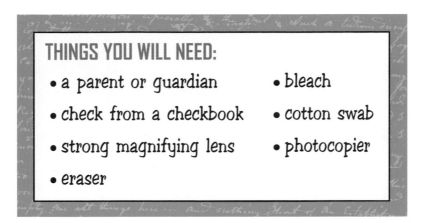

THINGS YOU WILL NEED:

- a parent or guardian
- check from a checkbook
- strong magnifying lens
- eraser
- bleach
- cotton swab
- photocopier

1 Ask a parent or guardian to help you with this experiment. You will need a check from their checkbook.

2 Examine the check. Notice how banks make it difficult to forge checks. Is the check colored? Examine the signature line with a strong magnifying lens. It probably has microprinting. Without magnification, it looks like a line.

3 What happens if you try to erase print on the check?

4 Ask the adult to swab a small drop of bleach over some print on the check. What happens?

5 Examine the security information on the back of the check. Photocopy both the front and back of the check. Does the security information appear when you photocopy the back of the check? What happens to the signature line when you photocopy the check?

Forging Checks

The most common forgery is signing another person's name (signature) on a check. Handwriting experts can usually spot this. Forgers sometimes try to erase letters or numbers. This damages the fibers. Changes in the fibers can be seen with a microscope. Chemicals, such as bleach, may be used to erase letters or numbers or enable someone to change them. However, the chemicals may discolor the check. If not, the changes can usually be seen in ultraviolet or infrared light. Shining the light from the side may make changes easier to see.

Forgers sometimes try to add value to a check. Figure 9 shows how a *9* can be changed to *90*, a *1* to a *7*, and *seven* to a *seventy*. Such changes are made with pen and ink. The ink may be different from the original ink. Infrared photographs may show that the inks are different even if the color appears to be the same.

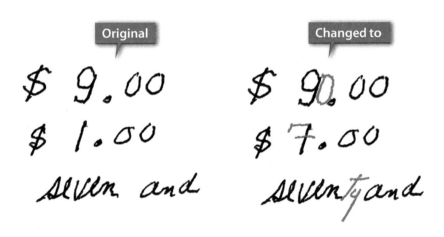

Figure 9. Some ways that criminals alter the amount on checks

Who Dunnit? A Crime to Solve

A bank has asked you to examine the check shown in Figure 10. The bank thinks a forger may have been at work. What do you think? What makes you think so? What would you do next? What should the bank do?

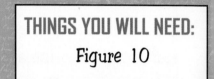

145

5-7017/2110
42

Sam Spade
20 Apple Lane
Happy City, USA 00000

Date _12/25/10_

$ _90,000_

Pay to the order of _John Doe_ ~~~~~~~~~~~~~~ Dollars

Ninety thousand ~~~~~~~~~~

Citizens Circle Account

CITIZENS BANK
Massachusetts

Sam Spade

For _services rendered_

Figure 10. Did someone commit forgery on this check?

Answers to Who Dunnit?

Crimes to Solve

1-3: Suspect 3 wrote the note. His handwriting matches the handwriting in the ransom note. For example, the direction of the slant is to the right. The letters *f*, *g*, and *l* have loops. There is space between letters in some words, such as "unarmed."

2-3: The ink matched that found in a Sheaffer fountain pen containing black ink.

This evidence alone could not prove the suspect was guilty. Police should try to get fingerprints from the pen and the written plan. A match of fingerprints would be better evidence. DNA from skin cells left on the pen and plan would be very convincing evidence.

3-3: The message, which was sent to "all members of the gang," reads:

Memo:

From: I. M. Robber

20 Robbers Lane

Crime City, CT 06000

Regarding Crime City First National Bank

To all members of the gang

The Plan

1. The guard goes for coffee at 10:30. Safe is open.
2. We hit the bank at 10:33. Wear masks. Carry guns.
3. Bob: Park car next to bank at 10:35.
4. Bill: Watch for cops at door.
5. Al: Get dough from tall teller.
6. Joe: Get all bank workers behind tall teller. Keep them covered.
7. I'll go into safe with bags, fill them and come out.
8. Bill: Cover us as we leave.
9. Go to our hideout.
10. Split the money and separate.

The note gives the address of I. M. Robber, the gang's leader. The police should go to his address and arrest him. It is likely that they will also recover some of the stolen money and perhaps some other members of the gang.

4-3: It appears that someone changed $9000 to $90,000 and nine to ninety. Tell the bank of the forgery. The bank will stop payment on the check and notify police.

Words to Know

chromatography—A method used to separate chemicals using paper and liquid.

counterfeit money—Money that has been illegally copied and printed and is not genuine.

crime scene—The place where a crime happened.

documents—Materials, usually paper, that have letters, numbers, or symbols that form a message. Documents are often written with ink, pencil, or print from a machine.

evidence—The things left behind or carried away from a crime scene. These things (fingerprints, hair, blood, ink, etc.) can be used to solve crimes and to convict criminals in a court of law.

feathering—The spreading of ink as it moves among unsized fibers.

forensic science—The science used to investigate and solve crimes. It is also used in courts of law.

forensic scientist—Someone who uses science to help solve crimes or to present as evidence in court.

forgery—Something such as a document or signature that is not genuine.

indented writing—Indentations (depressions) on a paper made by writing on a page on top of it.

infrared light—Light whose wavelength is longer than the red light we can see.

invisible ink—An ink that cannot be seen. It can be made visible by heating or treating the ink with a chemical.

microprinting—The very small writing on checks and money. You may need a magnifying glass to read it.

signature—A person's written name. It is a legal form of identification.

sizing—A gelatinous substance made of glue, wax, or clay. It is used to coat paper. It fills the spaces between the fibers, making the paper smooth.

ultraviolet light—Light whose wavelength is shorter than the violet light we can see.

watermark—A design impressed in paper during its manufacture. It can be seen when the paper is held up to the light.

Further Reading

Bardhan-Quallen, Sudipta. *Championship Science Fair Projects: 100 Sure-to-Win Experiments.* New York: Sterling Publishing, 2004.

Harris, Elizabeth Snoke. *Crime Scene Science Fair Projects.* New York: Lark Books, 2006.

Hopping, Lorraine Jean. *Crime Scene Science: Investigating a Crime Scene.* Milwaukee: World Almanac Library, 2007.

Rhadigan, Joe, and Rain Newcomb. *Prize-Winning Science Fair Projects for Curious Kids.* New York: Lark Books, 2004.

Internet Addresses

History Detectives Kids
<http://pbskids.org/historydetectives/index.html>

Who Dunnit?
<http://www.cyberbee.com/whodunnit/crime.html>

Index